KU-534-092

RUGBY

Wit

RUGBY WIT

First published in 2007
Reprinted 2009
This edition copyright © Summersdale Publishers Ltd, 2013

Illustrations © Ian Baker

All rights reserved.

No part of this book may be reproduced by any means, nor transmitted, nor translated into a machine language, without the written permission of the publishers.

Condition of Sale
This book is sold subject to the condition that it shall not, by way of trade or otherwise, be lent, re-sold, hired out or otherwise circulated in any form of binding or cover other than that in which it is published and without a similar condition including this condition being imposed on the subsequent purchaser.

Summersdale Publishers Ltd
46 West Street
Chichester
West Sussex
PO19 1RP
UK

www.summersdale.com

Printed and bound by CPI Group (UK) Ltd, Croydon, CR0 4YY

ISBN: 978-1-84953-460-4

Substantial discounts on bulk quantities of Summersdale books are available to corporations, professional associations and other organisations. For details contact Nicky Douglas by telephone: +44 (0) 1243 756902, fax: +44 (0) 1243 786300 or email: nicky@summersdale.com.

RUGBY

Wit

QUIPS AND
QUOTES FOR THE
RUGBY-OBSESSED

RICHARD BENSON

summersdale

CONTENTS

EDITOR'S NOTE

History has been kind to William Webb Ellis but few can testify what his teammates thought of him when on a wet day in 1823, with complete disregard for the rules of football, he picked up the ball and proceeded to run with it. In the annals of time, however, on that memorable day, he will be forever blessed with inventing the honourable, brutal, but always beautiful game of rugby.

Amongst these pages you will find timeless quotes and quips by players of the game, lovers of the game and observers of the game. Be they profound, funny or just plain rude they all have rugby, with all its foibles and intricacies, at their heart. It's only fair that a game that has brought so much joy, so much passion and so much fuel for argument be given a platform whereby its players and fans alike can pass on their wisdom and their foolishness for all fans of the game to enjoy.

THE ALL BLACKS

You can go to the end
of time, the last World
Cup in the history
of mankind, and the
All Blacks will be
favourites for it.

PHIL KEARNS, AUSTRALIAN RUGBY PLAYER

You actually need to see an All Blacks jersey out on the field, on the back of the man who has won the right to wear it, to appreciate its impact, its depth, its sheer, unadulterated blackness.

ANONYMOUS

The whole of the world is tribal, but when it comes to rugby, New Zealand is much more tribal than most. The All Blacks are the national virility symbol. Their people support them come hail, rain or shine.

MIKE GIBSON, NORTHERN IRISH RUGBY PLAYER

———— •◉• ————

We are not calling them the All Blacks this week. They are New Zealand. New Zealand is a poxy little island in the South Pacific.

SCOTT JOHNSON, AUSTRALIAN ASSISTANT
COACH FOR THE WALLABIES

Of course it worries me if the All Blacks are invincible. I mean, it stands to reason, if we can't see them, how can we beat them?

ANONYMOUS ENGLISH RUGBY PLAYER

———•••———

New Zealand are the best team in the world – the execution and accuracy of their skills were a lesson in modern rugby.

JOSH LEWSEY, ENGLISH RUGBY PLAYER

I am shattered, our dreams
were shattered and I feel
sick about it all.

JOHN HART, NEW ZEALAND RUGBY COACH,
AFTER FRANCE DEFEATED THE ALL BLACKS IN
THE 1999 WORLD CUP SEMI-FINAL

———•●•———

New Zealand rugby is a
colourful game since you
get all black... and blue.

ANONYMOUS

Subdue and penetrate.

ALL BLACKS CLUB MOTTO

———— •●• ————

The suspicion is growing that the All Blacks will not have to be sublime in France. They will just have to be there.

STEPHEN JONES, WELSH RUGBY PLAYER AND COACH, SIZING UP THE ALL BLACKS' CHANCES FOR THE 2007 WORLD CUP IN FRANCE

Mud, rain, blood, haka. It sounds like rugby heaven to me.

ANONYMOUS

———— •◆• ————

[It was] the first time I've ever felt like a boy in a man's body. I was absolutely shitting myself.

ZINZAN BROOKE, NEW ZEALAND RUGBY PLAYER, RECALLING HOW HE FELT RUNNING OUT WITH THE REST OF THE ALL BLACKS FOR THE FIRST MATCH OF THEIR 1992 SOUTH AFRICA TOUR AT KING'S PARK IN DURBAN

Foul play and cheating are the two factors that can make the game unplayable... the All Blacks are guilty of both.

CLEM THOMAS, WELSH RUGBY PLAYER

———•●•———

Five years ago, many of the England team were sick at half-time – such is the intensity of playing the All Blacks.

LAWRENCE DALLAGLIO, ENGLISH RUGBY PLAYER

ALL BRAWN, NO BRAINS

That kick was
absolutely unique,
except for the one
before it which
was identical.

TONY BROWN, NEW ZEALAND RUGBY PLAYER

It went well. There are no problems, and, as a bonus, it showed that I have a brain!

CORNÉ KRIGE, SOUTH AFRICAN RUGBY PLAYER, AFTER GOING FOR A BRAIN SCAN

———•●•———

You guys line up alphabetically by height and you guys pair up in groups of three, then line up in a circle.

COLIN COOPER, NEW ZEALAND RUGBY COACH

Nobody in
rugby should be
called a genius. A
genius is a guy like
Norman Einstein.

JONO GIBBES, NEW ZEALAND RUGBY PLAYER AND COACH

I told him, 'Son, what is it with you. Is it ignorance or apathy?' He said, 'David, I don't know and I don't care.'

DAVID NUCIFORA, AUSTRALIAN RUGBY PLAYER AND COACH, TALKING ABOUT TROY FLAVELL, NEW ZEALAND RUGBY PLAYER

—●●●—

I owe a lot to my parents, especially my mother and father.

TANA UMAGA, NEW ZEALAND RUGBY PLAYER

It's definitely the hardest tackle
I've taken in my life but I'm still
breathing and that's a good sign.

DERICK HOUGAARD, SOUTH AFRICAN RUGBY PLAYER

———— •●• ————

He's a guy who gets up at
six o'clock in the morning
regardless of what time it is.

COLIN COOPER, ON PAUL TITO, NEW ZEALAND RUGBY PLAYER

I want to reach for 150 or
200 points this season,
whichever comes first.

DAVID HOLWELL, NEW ZEALAND RUGBY PLAYER

Colin has done a bit of mental
arithmetic with a calculator.

MA'A NONU, NEW ZEALAND RUGBY PLAYER

It's not lost or anything,
we just don't exactly know
where it is at the moment.

DEREK SAMPSON, NEW ZEALAND MANAGER OF
THE BLUES, ON THE WHEREABOUTS OF THE NPC
TROPHY AFTER WINNING IT IN 2002

Most Misleading Campaign of
1991: England's rugby World Cup
squad, who promoted a scheme
called 'Run with the Ball'. Not,
unfortunately, among themselves.

TIME OUT, 1991

I've never had major knee surgery on any other part of my body.

JERRY COLLINS, NEW ZEALAND RUGBY PLAYER

BLAME THE REF:
EVERYONE ELSE DOES

Referees are only
human, I think.

PHIL KEARNS, AUSTRALIAN RUGBY PLAYER

I never comment on referees
and I'm not going to break the
habit of a lifetime for that prat.

EWEN MCKENZIE, AUSTRALIAN RUGBY PLAYER AND COACH

———•●●•———

I think you enjoy the game more
if you don't know the rules.
Anyway, you're on the same
wavelength as the referees.

JONATHAN DAVIES, WELSH RUGBY PLAYER

Get off, you look ugly.

PETER MARSHALL, AUSTRALIAN REFEREE, TO BLOOD-SPATTERED
NEIL BACK, ENGLISH RUGBY PLAYER, AFTER HE COMPLAINED
ABOUT BEING ORDERED TO THE BLOOD BIN IN ENGLAND'S
2003 WORLD CUP GAME AGAINST SOUTH AFRICA

The first half is invariably much
longer than the second. This
is partly because of the late
kick-off but is also caused by
the unfitness of the referee.

MICHAEL GREEN, AUTHOR AND BRITISH HUMORIST,
THE ART OF COARSE RUGBY

———•◦•———

Far be it for me to criticise the
referee but I saw him after the
match and he was heading straight
for the opticians. Guess who he
bumped into on the way? Everyone.

IAN 'MIGHTY MOUSE' MCLAUCHLAN, SCOTTISH RUGBY PLAYER

When a referee is in doubt, he is justified in deciding against the side which makes the most noise because they are probably wrong.

ANONYMOUS

———•••———

A lot of abuse directed at the ref is self-explanatory – or kept simple enough so he'll at least understand it.

JUSTIN BROWN, NEW ZEALAND AUTHOR, *RUGBY SPEAK*

Referees aren't paranoid –
everybody really does hate them.

IAIN SPRAGG, BRITISH AUTHOR

───────●●●───────

Grandmother or tails, sir?

ANONYMOUS RUGBY REFEREE TO PRINCESS ANNE'S SON
PETER PHILLIPS, GORDONSTOUN SCHOOL'S RUGBY CAPTAIN,
FOR HIS PRE-MATCH COIN-TOSS PREFERENCE IN 1995

───────●●●───────

I never wore a mouth guard,
hated them... too uncomfortable,
and besides, you couldn't
abuse the referee.

CLIFF WATSON, ENGLISH RUGBY PLAYER

Often, when they're supposed
to be focusing on the offside
or forward pass, they're really
thinking about shoe sales and
chocolate brownie recipes.

JUSTIN BROWN, *RUGBY SPEAK*

•◦•

If you're a ref and you want
the big appointments, you've
got to lick the backsides of
some of the top nations.

DAVE WATERSTON, NEW ZEALAND HEAD COACH
OF NAMIBIA'S NATIONAL RUGBY UNION TEAM

I have been sent off that many times that when I'm in the yard doing the gardening and the postman goes by and blows his whistle, I just get up and go have a shower.

NOEL KELLY, AUSTRALIAN RUGBY PLAYER AND COACH

———— •●• ————

Players and spectators at all levels can enjoy sport better if they totally accept two simple rules. Rule one: the referee is always right. Rule two: in the event of the referee being obviously wrong, rule one applies.

PETER CORRIGAN, SPORTS JOURNALIST

CELEBRITIES ON RUGBY

My drinking team has
a rugby problem.

OSCAR WILDE, IRISH PLAYWRIGHT, NOVELIST AND POET

Rugby is a game for big buggers;
if you're not a big bugger you get
hurt. I wasn't a big bugger but I
was a fast bugger and therefore
I avoided the big buggers.

SPIKE MILLIGAN, IRISH COMEDIAN

Rugby – posh man's sport,
of course. Fifteen men on a
team because posh people can
afford to have more friends.

AL MURRAY, ENGLISH COMEDIAN

Rugby is a game for the mentally deficient, that is why it was invented by the British. Who else but an Englishman could invent an oval ball?

PETER COOK, ENGLISH SATIRIST, WRITER AND COMEDIAN

———•●•———

[Rugby is] the most vicious sport on God's Earth.

CHRIS EUBANK, ENGLISH BOXER

I prefer rugby to soccer.
I enjoy the violence in
rugby, except when
they start biting each
other's ears off.

ELIZABETH TAYLOR, ENGLISH-AMERICAN ACTRESS

Rugby is a wonderful show.
Dance, opera and, suddenly,
the blood of a killing.

RICHARD BURTON, WELSH ACTOR

———— •●• ————

Playing rugby at school I once
fell on a loose ball and, through
ignorance and fear, held on despite
a fierce pummelling. After that
it took me months to convince
my teammates I was a coward.

PETER COOK

Sweden and rugby aren't
very good friends. I really
don't understand it.

SVEN-GÖRAN ERIKSSON, SWEDISH ENGLAND
NATIONAL FOOTBALL TEAM MANAGER

———— •●• ————

Rugby is a good occasion for
keeping 30 bullies far from
the centre of the city.

OSCAR WILDE

———— •●• ————

The women sit, getting colder
and colder, on a seat getting
harder and harder, watching oafs
getting muddier and muddier.

VIRGINIA GRAHAM, AMERICAN TV PRESENTER,
WRITER AND COMMENTATOR

CLASSIC COMMENTARY

Strangely, in slow
motion replay, the ball
seemed to hang in the
air for even longer.

MURRAY MEXTED, NEW ZEALAND TV COMMENTATOR

What a great-sounding name. He sounds like a drug dealer from Brazil.

MURRAY MEXTED, ON RICO GEAR, NEW ZEALAND RUGBY PLAYER

———•●•———

They trained like Tarzan all week and then played like Jane.

WAYNE SMITH, NEW ZEALAND RUGBY PLAYER AND COACH

You don't like to see
hookers going down
on players like that.

MURRAY MEXTED

He's like a mad ferret.

BILL MCLAREN, SCOTTISH RUGBY COMMENTATOR

———•◆•———

We want consistency, but we
don't want a consistent referee to
consistently blow the whistle.

MURRAY MEXTED

Andy Ellis – the 21 year old, who turned 22 a few weeks ago...

MURRAY MEXTED

———•●•———

Commentator: 'The Frenchman took a bit of a shoeing there, didn't he Brian?'
Brian Moore: 'I don't care, he's a Frenchman.'

AN ANONYMOUS COMMENTATOR AND BRIAN MOORE, ENGLISH RUGBY PLAYER, DURING AN RBS 6 NATIONS GAME BETWEEN FRANCE AND ENGLAND

There's nothing that a tight forward likes more than a loosie right up his backside.

MURRAY MEXTED

———●●●———

An easy kick for George Fairburn now but, as everybody knows, no kicks are easy.

DAVID DOYLE-DAVIDSON, BBC RADIO COMMENTATOR

That guy is so quick; he can
switch off the light and get into
bed before the room is dark.

JACK GIBSON, AUSTRALIAN RUGBY PLAYER AND COACH

———•●•———

Well, either side could win
it, or it could be a draw.

MURRAY MEXTED

I look at Colin Meads and see
a great big sheep farmer who
carried the ball in his hands as
though it was an orange pip.

BILL MCLAREN

———•●•———

The All Blacks second-rowers
are huge men. They're both over
one metre tall... hang on, that
would make them midgets.

MURRAY MEXTED

If Walt Disney had seen this
little man's antics, there'd
have been no Mickey Mouse.

RAY FRENCH, ENGLISH COMMENTATOR AND RUGBY PLAYER,
ON PETER STERLING, AUSTRALIAN RUGBY PLAYER

———•◦•———

Just watch the pace of the
French defence. They are
attacking the Irish defensively.

DAVID FORDHAM, AUSTRALIAN COMMENTATOR

———•◦•———

Sky TV Producer: 'Murray
can you hear me?... Murray
can you hear me?'
Murray Mexted: 'No.'

A SOUND CHECK BEFORE A SPRINGBOK TEST AT CARISBROOK

THE DRAGONS

Don't ask me about emotions in the Welsh dressing room. I'm someone who cries when he watches *Little House on the Prairie*.

BOB NORSTER, WELSH RUGBY PLAYER

Welsh rugby may be about as
healthy as a 40-a-day smoker with
a gammy leg and a whisky habit,
but Llanelli will be up for this.

CHRIS HEWETT, RUGBY UNION CORRESPONDENT, *THE INDEPENDENT*

———— •●• ————

Nobody ever beats Wales at rugby,
they just score more points.

GRAHAM MOURIE, NEW ZEALAND RUGBY PLAYER AND COACH

Growing up in Wales meant two things to me: rugby on a Saturday and chapel on Sunday. The thought of doing anything else just never crossed our minds as youngsters.

GARETH EDWARDS, WELSH RUGBY PLAYER

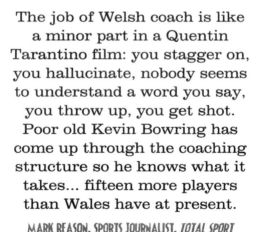

The job of Welsh coach is like a minor part in a Quentin Tarantino film: you stagger on, you hallucinate, nobody seems to understand a word you say, you throw up, you get shot. Poor old Kevin Bowring has come up through the coaching structure so he knows what it takes... fifteen more players than Wales have at present.

MARK REASON, SPORTS JOURNALIST, *TOTAL SPORT*

I knew he would never play
for Wales... he's tone deaf.

HUW DAVIES' FATHER, ON HIS SON'S CHOICE
TO PLAY RUGBY FOR ENGLAND

———•◦•———

Wales have always had it in
them to play this kind of no-
fear, high-velocity rugby, but
it's not an easy trick to pull off
if you haven't got the ball.

MARTIN JOHNSON, ENGLISH RUGBY PLAYER AND COACH

———•◦•———

I don't think they showed us
respect as a team – but I think
they will respect us now.

GRAHAM HENRY, NEW ZEALAND ALL BLACKS COACH AND
WALES NATIONAL RUGBY UNION TEAM COACH, AFTER THE
WELSH DEFEAT OF ENGLAND IN THE 1999 FIVE NATIONS

ENGLAND V WALES

The relationship between the Welsh and the English is based on trust and understanding. They don't trust us and we don't understand them.

DUDLEY WOOD, ENGLISH SECRETARY OF THE ENGLISH RFU

There is nothing quite like a
white shirt with a red rose on it
to motivate a Welsh rugby team,
and if the forwards indulged in
the time-honoured motivational
practice of butting the dressing-
room wall before taking the field,
the ferocity with which they
began the match (and indeed
finished it) suggested that the
gate receipts would only just
cover the plastering bill.

MARTIN JOHNSON, THE *DAILY TELEGRAPH*

—•◉•—

When it comes to the
One Great Scorer
To mark against your name
He'll ask not how you
played the game
But whether you beat England.

WELSH PROVERB

Look what these bastards have done to Wales. They've taken our coal, our water, our steel. They buy our houses and they only live in them for a fortnight every 12 months. What have they given us? Absolutely nothing. We've been exploited, raped, controlled and punished by the English – and that's who you are playing this afternoon.

PHIL BENNETT, WELSH RUGBY PLAYER, GIVING A PRE-GAME TALK TO THE WELSH TEAM BEFORE FACING ENGLAND

THE ENGLISH

Turn them over.
Smash 'em. Simple as
that. Relish this game.
Relish it. Shut their crowd
up, shut their players up.
Win the match.

MARTIN JOHNSON, BEFORE THE GRAND SLAM
DECIDER AGAINST IRELAND IN DUBLIN IN 2002

I was going nuts. We kept putting ourselves in trouble, making error after error. But who cares what I thought? We have won the World Cup.

SIR CLIVE WOODWARD, ENGLISH RUGBY PLAYER AND COACH

They were outstanding. They are the best team in the world by one minute.

EDDIE JONES, AUSTRALIAN RUGBY COACH, ON THE 2003 ENGLAND RUGBY TEAM

Of all the teams in the world you don't want to lose to, England's top of the list. If you beat them, it's because you cheat. If they beat you, it's because they've overcome your cheating.

GRANT FOX, NEW ZEALAND RUGBY PLAYER

———— •●• ————

We're going to tear those boys apart.

WILL CARLING, ENGLISH RUGBY PLAYER, PINNED THIS MESSAGE UP ON THE CHANGING-ROOM WALL BEFORE HIS TEAM RAN OUT TO FACE THE ALL BLACKS IN THE 1995 WORLD CUP SEMI-FINAL IN CAPE TOWN. IT ONLY TOOK 70 SECONDS FOR NEW ZEALAND TO SCORE THEIR FIRST TRY AS THEY DEMOLISHED ENGLAND 45-29.

The only thing you're ever likely to catch on the end of an English back line is chilblains.

DAVID CAMPESE, AUSTRALIAN RUGBY PLAYER

———•●•———

I will handle things the Brian Clough way. Whenever a player has a problem we will talk about it for 20 minutes and I will listen carefully to what he has to say. Then we'll agree that I was right.

SIR CLIVE WOODWARD

It was like the Falklands
crisis. I was counting them
in and counting them out.

JACK ROWELL, ENGLISH RUGBY COACH, ON HIS MULTI-PLAYER
INJURY SUBSTITUTIONS AGAINST WESTERN SAMOA IN 1995

Me? As England's answer
to Jonah Lomu? Joanna
Lumley, more likely.

DAMIAN HOPLEY, ENGLISH RUGBY PLAYER

I could hardly kiss him, could I? We did realise we were hugging each other for a little bit too long, though — and moved on to find someone else to do it to!

WILL GREENWOOD, ENGLISH RUGBY PLAYER, WHO WAS THE FIRST MAN INTO THE ARMS OF FELLOW ENGLISH PLAYER JONNY WILKINSON

He was like Luke Skywalker
in *Star Wars*, when he has
his hand lopped off and
keeps coming back again.

JEREMY GUSCOTT, ENGLISH RUGBY PLAYER,
ON JONNY WILKINSON'S RETURN TO THE
ENGLAND SIDE IN THE RBS 6 NATIONS

———— •❧• ————

The last thing we want to do is
to get too close to one another.
We don't want to get palsy-palsy.
But if we're going to have a live
session then let's have England
against France and let's go for it.

SIR CLIVE WOODWARD, ON THE PROSPECT OF
ENGLAND TRAINING WITH FRANCE

The only hope for the England rugby union team is to play it all for laughs. It would pack them in if the public address system at Twickenham was turned up full blast to record the laughs at every inept bit of passing, kicking or tackling. The nation would be in fits... and on telly the BBC would not need a commentator but just a tape of that laughing policeman, turning it loud at the most hilarious bits.

JIM RIVERS, LETTER TO *THE GUARDIAN*

———•●•———

London salutes you.

KEN LIVINGSTONE, ENGLISH MAYOR OF LONDON, PAID TRIBUTE TO ENGLAND'S RUGBY WORLD CUP WINNERS BY AWARDING THEM FREEDOM OF THE CITY OF GREATER LONDON IN 2003

They have this impression of English rugby that we all play in Wellington boots and we play in grass that is two foot long.

SIR CLIVE WOODWARD

●◉●

You might see some pommies running around in sandshoes rather than studded boots.

JOHN MUGGLETON, AUSTRALIAN RUGBY PLAYER AND COACH

FINAL WHISTLE

The time for
reminiscing is after
rugby. Then you can
sit down and get fat.

JOSH LEWSEY

I've always said I will play until
I am 30 and that is the target. I
would rather retire myself than
let someone else retire me.

CORNÉ KRIGE

The only trouble is my legs
are not as strong as they
were. I can't run any more.

GEORGE DANEEL, SOUTH AFRICAN RUGBY
PLAYER AND THE OLDEST SPRINGBOK

The heart is willing, the head is willing but the body's had enough.

KEITH WOOD, IRISH RUGBY PLAYER, ON HANGING UP HIS BOOTS

———●◆●———

I simply adore rugby and still feel excited every time I pull on a jersey. That I will miss, and so much more, but I'm sure rugby has prepared me well for real life.

THOMAS CASTAIGNÈDE, FRENCH RUGBY PLAYER, *THE GUARDIAN*, ON HIS ANNOUNCEMENT TO RETIRE FROM THE GAME AFTER THE 2007 WORLD CUP

I was this guy who'd been racing around down there, on that field in 1999, running straight over people, scoring tries, winning games, having fun. And I ended up so sick I couldn't even run past a little baby.

JONAH LOMU, NEW ZEALAND RUGBY PLAYER, TALKING ABOUT HIS KIDNEY DISORDER FROM WHICH HE RETURNED TO CONTINUE PLAYING

———•●●●•———

Being dropped and Take That splitting up on the same day is enough to finish anyone off.

MARTIN BAYFIELD, ENGLISH RUGBY PLAYER

My coaching reputation has probably gone up in smoke, but I really don't care. You want to cry for these guys. But at the end of the tournament I told them to go and get pissed and to be proud of themselves.

DAVE WATERSTON, AFTER NAMIBIA WERE
KNOCKED OUT OF THE 2003 WORLD CUP

Japan will give my body a chance to regenerate and hopefully by the time I'm 40 I'll still be able to run down the road.

JOSH BLACKIE, NEW ZEALAND RUGBY PLAYER, ON
MOVING TO JAPAN TO PLAY FOR THE KOBELCO STEELERS

FOR THE LOVE OF THE GAME

Rugby is just like love. You have to give before you can take. And when you give the ball it's like making love — you must think of the other's pleasure before your own.

SERGE BLANCO, FRENCH RUGBY PLAYER

The women and men who play
on that rugby field are more
alive than too many of us will
ever be. The foolish emptiness
we think we perceive in their
existence is only our own.

VICTOR CAHN, WRITER, *THE CHANGING ROOM*

———•●●•———

In this day and age of safety first,
of seatbelts, and cycle helmets,
low cholesterol butter, 'Warning:
Smoking is a Health Hazard' –
when so much is sanitised and
safe – the opportunity to feel that
sort of battle-knell thrill comes
less and less often. But it is there
in rugby, long may it remain.

PETER FITZSIMONS, AUSTRALIAN JOURNALIST AND WALLABY

Let me use an analogy. I have a Staffordshire bull-terrier. Every time I feed it osso buco, he eats it like it's his last meal, and I think I'm like, and the team's like, my Staffordshire bull-terrier. When it comes to meal times, that's how hungry, how passionate we are.

GEORGE GREGAN, AUSTRALIAN RUGBY PLAYER

It matters not whether you play on some rain-soaked, mist-cloaked, winter field in front of 200 spectators, or 10, or even none, or if you play in front of 70,000 spectators at Twickenham. The sensation is the same – an exhilaration of the body and soul that will forever linger in the minds of all who have known rugby.

FRED ALLEN, NEW ZEALAND RUGBY PLAYER AND COACH

Your throat is dry, your cheeks are burning, you feel breathless. All that stands between you and glory is an oval-shaped ball and a set of posts.

NEIL JENKINS, WELSH RUGBY PLAYER AND COACH, *LIFE AT NUMBER 10: AN AUTOBIOGRAPHY*

———•◉•———

Tiredness and fatigue is a mental thing. The body is capable of much, much more than most people think. I love rugby. I can't wait to play. Stay fresh mentally, work hard at something else, and rugby is a pleasure.

ANDRE VENTER, SOUTH AFRICAN RUGBY PLAYER

INTO POSITION

Props are as crafty
as a bag of weasels.

BILL MCLAREN

Look, these Phantom comic
swappers and Mintie eaters,
these blond-headed flyweights
are one thing, and we will need
them after the hard work's done.
But the real stuff's got to be
done right here by you blokes.

ROSS TURNBULL, AUSTRALIAN RUGBY PLAYER AND WALLABIES
MANAGER, TALKING TO THE WALLABY FORWARDS BEFORE
THEY PLAYED THE ALL BLACKS AT EDEN PARK IN 1978

I don't know why prop
forwards play rugby.

LIONEL WESTON, ENGLISH RUGBY PLAYER

You need a mental
toughness and
probably don't need
to be too bright.

MARK REGAN, ENGLISH RUGBY PLAYER,
ON PLAYING IN THE FRONT ROW

Forwards are the gnarled and scarred creatures who have a propensity for running into and bleeding all over each other.

PETER FITZSIMONS

⎯⎯⎯ ●●● ⎯⎯⎯

If I had been a winger, I might have been daydreaming and thinking about how to keep my kit clean for next week.

BILL BEAUMONT, ENGLISH RUGBY PLAYER

The backs preen themselves
and the forwards drink.

DEAN RICHARDS, ENGLISH RUGBY PLAYER

● ● ●

A good defender should be so mean
that if he owned the Atlantic Ocean
he still wouldn't give you a wave.

MORNE DU PLESSIS, SOUTH AFRICAN RUGBY PLAYER

The front row is an immensely technical place where brain and brawn collide; it is one which has fascinated me since I played a prop whose shorts caught fire during a game as a consequence of carrying a light for his half-time fag.

BILL LOTHIAN, SPORTS JOURNALIST, *EDINBURGH EVENING NEWS*

The touchline is the best defender.

ANONYMOUS

Playing in the second row doesn't require a lot of intelligence really.

BILL BEAUMONT

———•●•———

Rugby backs can be identified because they generally have clean jerseys and identifiable partings in their hair... Come the revolution the backs will be the first to be lined up against the wall and shot for living parasitically off the work of others.

PETER FITZSIMONS

Mothers keep
their photo on the
mantelpiece to stop
the kids going too
near the fire.

JIM NEILLY, NORTHERN IRISH SPORTS COMMENTATOR

Prop forwards don't get
Valentine's cards for religious
reasons – God made them ugly!

ANONYMOUS

———•◦•———

In 1823, William Webb Ellis first
picked up the ball in his arms
and ran with it. And for the
next 156 years forwards have
been trying to work out why.

TASKER WATKINS, WELSH PRESIDENT OF THE WELSH RFU

THE IRISH

The Irish treat you like royalty before and after the game, and kick you to pieces during it.

JEFF PROBYN, ENGLISH RUGBY PLAYER

It's a dismissive term to say the Irish team are plucky because it rings back to the old days when we went out and gave it a lash, set our hair on fire and ran after the opposition for 20 minutes and, if they survived that, they beat us by 50 points.

EDDIE O'SULLIVAN, IRISH RUGBY COACH

———— ●●● ————

Brian, what are you going to do for a face when Saddam wants his arse back?

PETER CLOHESSY, IRISH RUGBY PLAYER, TO BRIAN MOORE, DURING THE FIRST SCRUM OF THE ENGLAND V IRELAND MATCH IN TWICKENHAM IN 1994

Tony Ward is the most important rugby player in Ireland. His legs are far more important to his country than even those of Marlene Dietrich were to the film industry. A little hairier, maybe, but a pair of absolute winners.

C. M. H. GIBSON, IRISH RUGBY PLAYER, WALES V IRELAND 1979 MATCH PROGRAMME

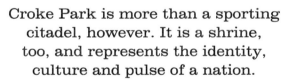

Croke Park is more than a sporting citadel, however. It is a shrine, too, and represents the identity, culture and pulse of a nation.

MARK SOUSTER, *THE TIMES*, BEFORE THE HISTORIC MATCH BETWEEN IRELAND AND FRANCE AT CROKE PARK, DUBLIN IN THE 2007 RBS 6 NATIONS

They can talk the talk, but they didn't walk the walk, did they?

RICHARD COCKERILL, ENGLISH RUGBY PLAYER, AFTER ENGLAND'S 1999 FIVE NATIONS VICTORY OVER IRELAND

———— •◉• ————

Dublin and Lansdowne Road stood out for me – many a good win and many a good night was had.

WILLIE JOHN MCBRIDE, NORTHERN IRISH RUGBY PLAYER AND COACH, REFLECTING ON HIS CAREER

———— •◉• ————

I didn't know what was going on at the start in the swirling wind. The flags were all pointing in different directions and I thought the Irish had starched them just to fool us.

MIKE WATKINS, WELSH RUGBY PLAYER, ON PLAYING FOR WALES AT LANSDOWNE ROAD, DUBLIN IN 1984

LEGENDS OF THE GAME

Bloody typical, isn't it?
The car's a write-off.
The tanker's a write-off. But JPR comes out
of it all in one piece.

GARETH EDWARDS, AFTER TEAMMATE J. P. R. WILLIAMS
WAS INVOLVED IN A ROAD TRAFFIC ACCIDENT

I'm still an amateur, of course,
but I became rugby's first
millionaire five years ago.

DAVID CAMPESE

———•••———

The bone was out of place and
I could feel something wasn't
right. Fortunately, a few moments
later I went in to tackle Hull's
Steve Norton and my jaw caught
his knee. The impact caused
my jaw to click back into place
and I was able to carry on.

ROGER MILLWARD, ENGLISH RUGBY PLAYER

I love an inner calm, a coolness,
a detachment; a brilliance
and insouciance which is
devastating. Some sniff the
wind – they created it.

CARWYN JAMES, WELSH RUGBY PLAYER AND COACH,
ON LIONS PLAYERS GERALD DAVIES AND BARRY JOHN

———•••———

I'm going to leave it to the new
generation, to the crash-it-up
robots that dominate the game.

DAVID CAMPESE

———•••———

Youngsters need heroes. They
need figures like Batman,
Tarzan and Naas Botha.

ABE MALAN, SOUTH AFRICAN RUGBY PLAYER

His sidestep was marvellous
– like a shaft of lightning.

BILL MCLAREN, ON WELSH RUGBY PLAYER GERALD DAVIES

———— •●● ————

You know exactly what he's
going to do. He's going to come
off his right foot at great speed.
You also know that there isn't a
blind thing you can do about it.

DAVID DUCKHAM, ENGLISH RUGBY PLAYER, ON GERALD DAVIES

Gary should have his own comic
strip in *The Victor* or *The Hotspur*.
He's just an ordinary bloke,
a lorry driver, and yet when
he pulls on a rugby shirt, he
becomes this sporting superhero.
He's simply outstanding.

JIM TELFER, SCOTTISH RUGBY PLAYER AND COACH,
ON GARY ARMSTRONG, SCOTTISH RUGBY PLAYER

———●●●———

A figure who inspires hero
worship among even those who
think a fly-half is a glass of
beer consumed when 'er indoors
is looking the other way.

ROBERT PHILIP, SPORTS JOURNALIST,
ON JONAH LOMU, THE *DAILY TELEGRAPH*

LES BLEUS

The French are predictably unpredictable.

ANDREW MEHRTENS, NEW ZEALAND RUGBY
PLAYER, AFTER AN ALL BLACKS SURPRISE LOSS TO
THE FRENCH IN THE 1999 RUGBY WORLD CUP

Long after the match, when the
stadium was dark, we all went
out onto the pitch. We did a lap
of honour, and we sang! We sang
Basque songs for half an hour.

SERGE BLANCO, ON THE FRENCH TEAM'S
CELEBRATION AFTER DEFEATING AUSTRALIA IN
THE SEMI FINALS OF THE 1987 WORLD CUP

———•●•———

They always lose when it matters.

BERNARD LAPORTE, FRENCH RUGBY COACH, GETTING IT
WRONG ABOUT ENGLAND IN THE WORLD CUP FINAL 2003

We will play well today.
Or maybe we'll play
well tomorrow, we
really don't know.

FRENCH RUGBY FEDERATION

If you can't take a punch, you should play table tennis.

PIERRE BERBIZIER, FRENCH RUGBY PLAYER AND COACH

———————•●•———————

In the end at Twickenham, unlike at Waterloo, it was France who pounded longest – and hardest – as they lowered England's colours to bring the chariot to a shuddering halt.

THE SUNDAY TIMES, ON ENGLAND'S LATE BREAKDOWN AGAINST FRANCE IN THE 1997 FIVE NATIONS

As far as the English are
concerned, I have decided to
adopt the same attitude as them:
I despise them as much as they
despise everybody else. And
as long as we beat England, I
wouldn't mind if we lost every
other game in the 6 Nations.

IMANOL HARINORDOQUY, BEFORE FRANCE'S MATCH
AGAINST ENGLAND IN THE 2003 RBS 6 NATIONS

———•●●•———

We French score tries because
we cannot kick penalties.

JEAN-PIERRE RIVES, FRENCH RUGBY PLAYER

We should have killed them
off in the first half but
didn't and paid for it.

BERNARD LAPORTE, AFTER FRANCE LOST TO
WALES IN THE 2005 RBS 6 NATIONS

We didn't only lose the semi-
final of the World Cup, we
lost a complete generation
of players. It was the end of
that team. It felt like the sky
had fallen in on our heads.

PHILIPPE SAINT-ANDRÉ, FRENCH RUGBY PLAYER AND COACH
AFTER FRANCE'S 1995 WORLD CUP LOSS TO SOUTH AFRICA

I think the French always niggle,
grabbing blokes around the balls
and the eyes and that sort of thing.

TIM LANE, AUSTRALIAN RUGBY PLAYER AND COACH

———•◦•———

The only memories I have of
England and the English are
unpleasant ones. They are so
chauvinistic and arrogant.

IMANOL HARINORDOQUY, FRENCH RUGBY PLAYER

LOOKING GOOD

It takes two hours
to get ready – hot
bath, shave my legs
and face, moisturise,
put fake tan on and
do my hair – which
takes a bit of time.

GAVIN HENSON, WELSH RUGBY PLAYER

Giant gargoyles, raw-boned,
cauliflower-eared monoliths
that intimidated and unsettled.
When they ran onto the field
it was like watching a tribe of
white orcs on steroids. Forget
their hardness, has there ever
been an uglier forward pack?

MICHAEL LAWS, NEW ZEALAND POLITICIAN,
BROADCASTER AND COLUMNIST, ON THE 2003 ENGLAND
PACK THAT WOULD LATER WIN THE WORLD CUP

———— •••• ————

Rugby players are like lava lamps:
good to look at but not very bright.

ANONYMOUS

———— •••• ————

The rugger is an unlikely sex
symbol – a hybrid of jock, bear,
and the guy who might have
beaten you up in high school.

CHRISTOPHER STAHL, JOURNALIST, *THE VILLAGE VOICE*

He looks successful, regimented, invincible, and stuffed with certainties. It fulfils a stereotype of the classic English Man, the rugger bugger.

SIMON HATTENSTONE, JOURNALIST,
THE GUARDIAN, ON JONNY WILKINSON

———•●●•———

It's because of rugby I've got dodgy ears.

PHIL GREENING, ENGLISH RUGBY PLAYER

———•●●•———

As you run around Battersea Park in them, looking like a cross between a member of the SAS and Blake's Seven, there is always the lingering fear of arrest.

BRIAN MOORE, ON THE ENGLAND NATIONAL RUGBY
UNION TEAM'S 1995 RUBBER TRAINING SUIT

LOSING

If at first you don't
succeed, find out if the
loser gets anything.

BILL LYON, AMERICAN SPORTS COLUMNIST

Rugby players may fall
in defeat but they will
never kneel for mercy.

ANONYMOUS

———●●●———

We've lost seven of our last
eight matches. Only team that
we've beaten was Western
Samoa. Good job we didn't
play the whole of Samoa.

GARETH DAVIES, ENGLISH RUGBY PLAYER

No leadership, no ideas. Not even enough imagination to thump someone in the line-up when the ref wasn't looking.

J. P. R. WILLIAMS, WELSH RUGBY PLAYER, ON WALES LOSING 28-9 AGAINST AUSTRALIA IN 1984

———•●●•———

I feel like I am the captain of the *Titanic*.

DAVE WATERSTON, AFTER HIS NAMIBIAN TEAM LOST 142-0 TO AUSTRALIA IN THE 2003 WORLD CUP

We actually got the winning
try three minutes from the
end but then they scored.

PHIL WAUGH, AUSTRALIAN RUGBY PLAYER

———•●•———

I don't know about us not
having a Plan B when things
went wrong, we looked like
we didn't have a Plan A.

GEOFF COOKE, ENGLISH RUGBY COACH, AFTER
ENGLAND HAD BEEN HUMBLED BY NEW ZEALAND
IN THE 1995 WORLD CUP SEMI-FINAL

Don't underestimate it, and
don't assume it's a matter
of simply going straight up.
That would be naive and
disrespectful to the opposition.

STUART LANCASTER, ENGLISH DIRECTOR OF LEEDS TYKES, GIVING
ADVICE TO TEAMS RELEGATED TO NATIONAL LEAGUE ONE

———————•●●•———————

It's bloody horrendous in League
One, all graft and no fun.

DREW HICKEY, AUSTRALIAN RUGBY PLAYER

Ultimately you get what
you deserve and we
deserved what we got.

PAUL GRAYSON, ENGLISH RUGBY PLAYER AND COACH

———•○•———

This hasn't been a very nice
experience – I've got to slink home
now in disguise because I still
live in Bath. We got a stuffing.

RICHARD HILL, ENGLISH RUGBY PLAYER AND COACH

'If only' are the two most useless words ever uttered by sportsmen after a defeat but no matter how useless they are we still keep using them.

ROB ANDREW, ENGLISH RUGBY PLAYER, AFTER ENGLAND WAS CRUSHED BY NEW ZEALAND 45–29 IN THE 1995 WORLD CUP SEMI-FINALS

———•◆•———

What hurts me most is some people will lose their jobs and that's hard to take. But the world keeps turning.

PAUL GRAYSON, ON RELEGATION

OFF THE PITCH

It was not possible for my players to turn the other cheek, as that was being punched as well.

EDDIE JONES, WELSH MANAGER OF PONTYPRIDD RFC,
ON THE 25-MINUTE BARROOM BRAWL AFTER THEIR
1997 HEINEKEN CUP GAME AGAINST BRIVE

I'm just off for a quiet pint;
followed by 15 noisy ones.

GARETH CHILCOTT, ENGLISH RUGBY PLAYER,
AFTER HIS LAST GAME FOR BATH

———•●•———

We've been together three and
a half days and we haven't
been to the pub yet.

DONAL LENIHAN, IRISH RUGBY PLAYER AND MANAGER
OF THE BRITISH LIONS, ON THE DIFFERENCE BETWEEN THE
PROFESSIONAL 2001 LIONS AND HIS 1989 SQUAD

I yell and scream like they do.
I'm the worst of them. Totally.
I'm a nightmare. Once they
gave me the passport that was
it – I started throwing my hands
in the air, drinking red wine
and flying off the handle.

JOHN KIRWAN, NEW ZEALAND RUGBY COACH, ON LIFE IN ITALY

———— •◆• ————

The use of video evidence is
not always conclusive, but
it sure beats the memory
bank of most witnesses.

JACK GIBSON

All three Tests will be televised and I've already re-arranged the lounge room so my armchair is at the front.

LARRY DEVINE, NEW ZEALAND FATHER
OF ALL BLACK STEVE DEVINE

— ●●● —

I've got a bottle of Johnnie Walker Blue. I'm going to consult it tonight and come up with a plan.

DAVE WATERSTON, FOLLOWING NAMIBIA'S LOSS
TO ARGENTINA IN THE 2003 WORLD CUP AND
PREPARING TO FACE THE WALLABIES

I'm pleased to say I don't think about rugby all the time: just most of the time.

LAWRENCE DALLAGLIO

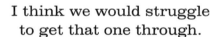

I think we would struggle to get that one through.

EDDIE JONES, ON THE NEWS THAT SOUTH AFRICA WILL SUBJECT THEIR PLAYERS TO A 'NO WOMEN, NO ALCOHOL' POLICY DURING THE WORLD CUP

People think rugby players
would make the worst dancers
but you would be surprised.
Some moves we use to warm
up are similar to dancing.

MATT DAWSON, ENGLISH RUGBY PLAYER, *THE SUN*

———•●●•———

The spirit was excellent. Yes, we
were all naked together at times,
but so what? The only chaps who
were perhaps a bit shy initially
were those with small willies.
At times, we ourselves asked if
we could strip off our clothes.

UNNAMED SOUTH AFRICAN RUGBY PLAYER AFTER THE MEDIA
REVELATIONS ABOUT 2003 WORLD CUP SQUAD TRAINING
CAMP, KAMP STAALDRAAD, SOUTH AFRICA'S *THE STAR*

ON THE PITCH

The first half will be
even. The second half
will be even harder.

TERRY HOLMES, WELSH RUGBY PLAYER

We can beat Ireland.

PIERRE BERBIZIER, AHEAD OF A CRUCIAL RBS 6 NATIONS GAME WITH IRELAND. FINAL SCORE: ITALY, 24; IRELAND, 51

It's like when two boxers come together. Some boxers find it difficult against opponents that you would ordinarily expect them to find it straightforward against.

FRANK HADDEN, SCOTTISH RUGBY COACH

Get your retaliation in first.

CARWYN JAMES

———•●•———

We must set our marker down
early defensively, not sitting
back waiting to see what they
do. We need to knock people
over and once we do that our
game ticks over pretty well.

EDDIE O'SULLIVAN

In one match last year eight
water-bottle runners ran on
the field and gave drinks to
the players when someone was
injured in the first 30 seconds of
the game. Thirty seconds – hell
they must have been thirsty.
When I played we got a piece
of orange at halftime, and if
you were quick you got two.

COLIN MEADS

⎯⎯⎯⎯⎯•●•⎯⎯⎯⎯⎯

I suppose you can say I am
a bit old school. I expect the
players to go onto the field
expecting to play a full game.

KEVIN PUTT, SOUTH AFRICAN RUGBY COACH

I like to get in one really good tackle early in the game, even if it is late.

RAY GRAVELL, WELSH RUGBY PLAYER

Today we're going to do it
simple: forwards forward,
fullbacks behind!

ANONYMOUS COACH

The tactical difference between
association football and rugby with
its varieties seems to be that in the
former, the ball is the missile, in
the latter, men are the missiles.

ALFRED E. CRAWLEY, AUTHOR, *THE BOOK OF THE BALL*

Ray Gravell Eats Soft Centres.

BANNER AT CARDIFF ARMS PARK, 1970

We give up positions too easily in the first 10–15 minutes and then start the engines up. I'd rather we started the engines up at kick-off.

EDDIE O'SULLIVAN

Throughout the week I have one side of me that does all the preparation and resting and eating well and training, then it hands all that over to the second individual, and that other individual is a hugely competitive, instinctive one who is just desperate to win. He is a bit of a monster, actually.

JONNY WILKINSON, ENGLISH RUGBY PLAYER, *THE GUARDIAN*

If the team don't score a
lot against us then we have
a chance of winning.

ANONYMOUS

———●●●———

Once you're on the pitch, it's
chaos. I find it faintly amusing,
this view that some people have
of the captain, clicking his fingers
and saying, 'Guys, let's try plan
B' and everyone goes, 'Oh God,
yes, plan B'. That's bollocks.

WILL CARLING, *THE INDEPENDENT*

PHILOSOPHICAL RUGBY

The whole point of
rugby is that it is, first
and foremost, a state
of mind, a spirit.

JEAN-PIERRE RIVES

Rugby is not like tea, which
is good only in England, with
English water and English milk.
On the contrary, rugby would be
better, frankly, if it were made in
a Twickenham pot and warmed
up in a Pyrenean cauldron.

DENNIS LALANNE, FRENCH WRITER

———•◦•———

Never a step backward.

MELBOURNE RUGBY CLUB MOTTO

Talent is secondary to whether
players are confident.

JACK GIBSON

———•●•———

Rugby football is a game for
gentlemen in all classes, but for
no bad sportsman in any class.

BARBARIANS FOOTBALL CLUB MOTTO

Rugby players are
either piano shifters
or piano movers.
Fortunately, I am
one of those who
can play a tune.

PIERRE DANOS, FRENCH RUGBY PLAYER

Life's a game, rugby is serious.

ANONYMOUS

———●●●———

All we're doing effectively is
chasing a pig's bladder around
a field, but we still have the
ability to touch so many people.

JOSH LEWSEY

I'd rather hit the ball
than be the ball.

HENNIE LE ROUX, SOUTH AFRICAN RUGBY PLAYER, ON
PREFERRING GOLF TO THE PROSPECT OF COACHING RUGBY

———————•●•———————

What makes rugby so special
is that there is always room
for the smaller man.

CONOR O'SHEA, IRISH DIRECTOR OF ACADEMIES
OF THE ENGLISH RFU, *THE GUARDIAN*

PLAYERS ON PLAYERS

[He's] the kind of
player you expect to
see emerging from
a ruck with the
remains of a jockstrap
between his teeth.

ANTHONY 'TONY' O'REILLY, IRISH RUGBY PLAYER
AND CURRENT CHAIRMAN OF THE INDEPENDENT
NEWS AND MEDIA GROUP, ON COLIN MEADS

I'm sure the lads will be glad to
see him gone. There'll be more
food for everyone else now!

AUSTIN HEALEY, ENGLISH RUGBY PLAYER,
ON JASON LEONARD'S RETIREMENT

• ● •

I've broken my nose this year and
I put my teeth all the way through
my lip. This is not good for my
modelling career. I said to Nobby:
How can I be a TV presenter
when my face looks like yours?

ROBBIE PAUL, NEW ZEALAND RUGBY PLAYER, ON
BRIAN NOBLE, ENGLISH RUGBY PLAYER AND COACH

Dean Richards is nicknamed
Warren, as in Warren ugly bastard.

JASON LEONARD, ENGLISH RUGBY PLAYER, ON HIS TEAMMATE

I've seen a lot people like him, but
they weren't playing on the wing.

COLIN MEADS, NEW ZEALAND RUGBY PLAYER, ON JONAH LOMU

I think Brian Moore's gnashers
are the kind you get from a DIY
shop and hammer in yourself. He
is the only player we have who
looks like a French forward.

PAUL RENDALL, ENGLISH RUGBY PLAYER, ON HIS TEAMMATE

———————•●•———————

It felt like I had run into
a brick shithouse.

THINUS DELPORT, SOUTH AFRICAN RUGBY PLAYER, ON
BEING TACKLED BY ALL BLACK, JERRY COLLINS

He moves with the
elegance of a cow
on a bicycle.

FRANK HYDE, AUSTRALIAN COMMENTATOR AND
RUGBY PLAYER, TALKING ABOUT NOEL KELLY

Fijian full-back, Waisele Serevi,
thinks 'tackle' is something
you take fishing with you.

JONATHAN DAVIES

———————•●•———————

I would have liked nothing
more than to knock him out.

CORNÉ KRIGE, ON MATT DAWSON

Will Carling epitomises England's lack of skills. He has speed and bulk but plays like a castrated bull.

DAVID CAMPESE

———•●•———

It does add a bit of spice that it is Leeds and it's quite fitting that I'll be playing in my good friend Barrie McDermott's last game. I'd like to ruin it for him.

ADRIAN MORLEY, ENGLISH RUGBY PLAYER

I've never seen
thighs that big before.

KENNY LOGAN, ON FIJIAN WINGER, RUPENI CAUCAUNIBUCA

— • • • —

One person has to slow him
down, a second has to knock
him over. He's young, naive,
and we'll put pressure on him.

WILL CARLING ON JONAH LOMU

— • • • —

There's no doubt about
it, he's a big bastard.

GAVIN HASTINGS ON JONAH LOMU

PLAYING WITH POLITICS

My favourite sport at
school was rugby. All
sports are teamwork,
but rugby particularly
is about teamwork and
I think teamwork is
the essence of this.

GORDON BROWN, BRITISH PRIME MINISTER

In the collective memory of this country rugby will always hold a place of pride for the role it played in nation building during those first years of our new democracy.

NELSON MANDELA, SOUTH AFRICAN PRESIDENT

———— •●• ————

World rugby has had a century of Lions tours, of invincible All Blacks and rampaging Springboks and where is the game of rugby in Honduras, Nepal and Egypt? Exactly where it was 100 years ago is probably pretty close to the answer.

PIO BOSCO TIKOISUVA, FIJIAN CHIEF EXECUTIVE OF THE FIJI RUGBY UNION

Every moment paled into insignificance when Mandela came in wearing a Springbok jersey and with South Africa winning the final, it defined so much more of what the potential of sport can be; a healer.

JOHN EALES, AUSTRALIAN RUGBY PLAYER

———————•◦•———————

It's like turkeys voting for Christmas.

ALAN SOLOMONS, SOUTH AFRICAN RUGBY COACH, ON SOUTH AFRICAN RUGBY ADMINISTRATORS

I am prepared to back David
depending on what his views are.

GLANMOR GRIFFITHS, WELSH CHAIRMAN OF THE WELSH RFU,
ON THE APPOINTMENT OF DAVID MOFFETT AS CHIEF EXECUTIVE

●◦●

All I ask is that when people
object to my ways is that they
stab me in the front not the back.

DAVID MOFFETT, WELSH CHIEF EXECUTIVE OF
THE WELSH RFU, ON HIS APPOINTMENT

If the game is run properly as
a professional game, you do not
need 57 old farts running rugby.

WILL CARLING

A bomb under the West car park at
Twickenham on an international
day would end fascism in
England for a generation.

PHILIP TOYNBEE, ENGLISH WRITER AND JOURNALIST

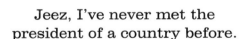

Jeez, I've never met the
president of a country before.

MALCOLM O'KELLY, IRISH RUGBY PLAYER, WHILE
NAKED IN THE DRESSING ROOM AFTER MEETING
AUSTRALIAN PRIME MINISTER JOHN HOWARD

RUGBY WARFARE

I couldn't very well
hit him could I? I had
the ball in my hands.

TOMMY BISHOP, ENGLISH RUGBY PLAYER, WHEN HE WAS
QUESTIONED ABOUT HIS KICKING OF A FELLOW PLAYER

It will not be a Korean war,
nor a Boer war, nor any other
war. It will be 15 men against
15, it will be professionals
against professionals.

GIDEON SAM, SOUTH AFRICAN RUGBY MANAGER

• • •

I mean we are lucky – people go to
Iraq. He's not getting killed... well
only for 80 minutes now and again.

MAILE FALEKAKALA, GIRLFRIEND OF MOSES RAULUNI,
FIJIAN RUGBY PLAYER, ON THE RISKS HE TAKES

In rugby there are no
winners, only survivors.

ANONYMOUS

———— •●● ————

South Africa were a disgrace.
Corné Krige as captain targeted
the entire England team. It
was all rather Jurassic.

STUART BARNES, ENGLISH COMMENTATOR AND RUGBY PLAYER

The convicts will smash the toffs.

DAVID CAMPESE

———— •●• ————

A player of ours has been
proven guilty of biting. That's
a scar that will never heal.

ANDY ROBINSON, ENGLISH RUGBY PLAYER AND COACH

For an 18-month suspension, I feel I probably should have torn it off. Then at least I could say, 'Look, I've returned to South Africa with the guy's ear.'

JOHAN LE ROUX, SOUTH AFRICAN RUGBY PLAYER, ON TAKING A BITE OUT OF SEAN FITZPATRICK, NEW ZEALAND RUGBY PLAYER

If you're being poked in the eye or punched in the nose, you act accordingly. Some back off, some go for the blood.

SCOTT GIBBS, WELSH RUGBY PLAYER

Eighty minutes, 15 positions,
no protection... wanna ruck?

ANONYMOUS

— • ● • —

One of the first things to
understand about rugby is that
it is a violent game, sometimes
it is extremely violent. While
violence isn't the point (as it
is in boxing or, say, hurling)
it is integral to the game.

DAVID KIRK, NEW ZEALAND RUGBY PLAYER, *BLACK AND BLUE*

You can't play well without suffering it, or being prepared to administer it. I'd go so far as to say that the team who can control their violence and apply it most effectively is the team that is likely to win.

DAVID KIRK, *BLACK AND BLUE*

———— •●• ————

When he moved away and I saw the blood streaming from the eye, I thought, 'Oh God, I could be in trouble here.'

MARTIN JOHNSON

Thou shalt not hesitate at the breakdown, but be mighty to get your rightful ball; for though it is written that the meek shall inherit the earth, this truly was a poor translation. The meek shall be trampled into the dirt is more to the point.

ANONYMOUS

It was blood-curdling stuff, and English blood was curdled to the point where it all drained into their boots.

MARTIN JOHNSON, *THE DAILY TELEGRAPH*

Rugby players have numbers on their jerseys because the coroner can't always identify the bodies by the dental records alone.

ANONYMOUS

At baseball games they play
organs, at rugby games
they donate organs.

ANONYMOUS

And there we see the sad
sight of Martin Offiah limping
off with a broken finger.

RAY FRENCH

RULES ARE MADE TO BE BROKEN

The advantage law is
the best law in rugby,
because it lets you
ignore all the others for
the good of the game.

DEREK ROBINSON, BRITISH AUTHOR

There is far too much talk about good ball and bad ball. In my opinion, good ball is when you have possession and bad ball is when the opposition have it.

DICKIE JEEPS, ENGLISH RUGBY PLAYER

———— •●• ————

Offside – a natural break in the play called by the referee every 35 seconds to let everyone get their breath back.

ANONYMOUS

You cheat and cheat until you get caught out and then you cheat some more, you've really got to play on that edge.

BRENT COCKBAIN, WELSH RUGBY PLAYER

———•●•———

Half of the game of rugby is learning the rules, the other half is learning how to cheat.

ANONYMOUS

Thou should not kiss thy teammate
on the mouth when he scores; for
such is an abomination unto God,
especially kisses in tongues, unless
you play football with the round
white ball and thus it is expected.

ANONYMOUS

———•◉•———

Thou shalt not chip nor kick for
touch if thou be a prop or wear any
jersey number below that of 7; for
this is an abomination unto the
Coach, and surely you will be his
at training, perhaps everlasting.

ANONYMOUS

THE SCOTS

Spy on Scotland?
What for?

DJURO SEN, AUSTRALIAN SPOKESMAN FOR THE
WALLABIES, ON ALLEGATIONS THAT THEY HAD
SECRETLY FILMED THEIR OPPONENTS IN TRAINING

There is no man more respected for his abilities both on and off the field than this delightful Scot, who is the epitome of the rugby man; brave, resolute, adventurous and one who loves a party.

CLEM THOMAS, ON GAVIN HASTINGS

———— •●• ————

I loved the Scots. Little Jimmy Renwick making a mockery of the centre stereotype... Deans throws, Tomes palms... John Rutherford and that sidestep. I always had a soft spot for Scotland.

ALEX GOFF, AMERICAN RUGBY JOURNALIST

Just like Scotland being gallant losers, we shouldn't apologise for winning, someone said we got out of jail, but who cares, we won.

SIMON TAYLOR, SCOTTISH RUGBY PLAYER, ON A NARROW 22-20 WIN OVER FIJI

———————•●●•———————

Scotland is the Pacific nation of Britain.

VA'AIGA TUIGAMALA, SAMOAN RUGBY PLAYER

———————•●●•———————

Saturday March 17, 1990, is one of those dates that's engraved in my mind like it was put there with a hammer and chisel. Grand Slam Saturday – the best day of my rugby life. It was the day of the underdog...

GARY ARMSTRONG, SCOTTISH RUGBY PLAYER ON SCOTLAND'S HISTORIC DEFEAT OF HOT FAVOURITES ENGLAND IN THE GRAND SLAM DECIDER AT MURRAYFIELD

The French pulled
up the Scots' kilts
and discovered they
had no balls.

ZINZAN BROOKE

THE GOOD, THE BAD AND THE UGLY

The Good

American football is rugby after a visit from a health and safety inspector.

ANONYMOUS

I love rugby because it's a socio-cultural experience; travelling the world and meeting people from different backgrounds... actually it's more for the frequent flyer points.

JAMES HOLBECK, AUSTRALIAN RUGBY COACH AND PLAYER

———— •●•● ————

[Rugby] players can achieve greatness even in the absence of silky skills and talent because they are deeply courageous, indomitable of spirit, great leaders and can make up for technical shortages.

STEPHEN JONES, *THE SUNDAY TIMES*

The only pain in
rugby is regret.

ANONYMOUS

The Bad

Sure there have been injuries
and deaths in rugby – but
none of them serious.

JOHN 'DOC' MAYHEW, DOCTOR TO THE NEW
ZEALAND NATIONAL RUGBY UNION TEAM

———•••———

I can't rest until I have tamed
the devil in my head.

JONNY WILKINSON, *THE GUARDIAN*

Rugby may have many problems, but the gravest is undoubtedly that of the persistence of summer.

CHRIS LAIDLAW, NEW ZEALAND WRITER, RADIO TALK-SHOW HOST AND RUGBY PLAYER, *MUD IN YOUR EYE: A WORM'S EYE VIEW OF THE CHANGING WORLD OF RUGBY*

———— •••• ————

We're showing signs of getting better. It's just a pity the tournament is over now.

KENNY LOGAN, SCOTTISH RUGBY PLAYER

People forget your good games, but the minute you have a bad game everyone remembers.

FAAN RAUTENBACH, SOUTH AFRICAN RUGBY PLAYER

———•●•———

Hell, it's been hard. I never thought it would be this bad. You have to be in it to experience it.

HARRY VILJOEN, SOUTH AFRICAN RUGBY COACH

The Ugly

Rugby people. Can't live with them. Can't shoot them.

TOM HUMPHRIES, SPORTS JOURNALIST, *THE TIMES*

●●●

Two sausages at tonight's barbeque please.

PHIL KEARNS TO NEW ZEALAND'S SEAN FITZPATRICK AFTER BARGING PAST HIM TO SCORE A TRY AND THEN MAKING A TWO-FINGERED HAND GESTURE

I may not have been very tall or very athletic, but the one thing I did have was the most effective backside in world rugby.

JIM GLENNON, IRISH POLITICIAN AND RUGBY PLAYER

———•●•———

The winger resembles Mother Brown, running with a high knee-lift and sometimes not progressing far from the spot where he started.

MARK REASON, ON SIMON GEOGHEGAN,
IRISH RUGBY PLAYER, *TOTAL SPORT*

———•●•———

Rugby is like turkey. Without chestnuts it's crude.

ERIC POUTAL, ARTIST

Rugby people have always
been college scarves and
jutting jaws and silly songs
I don't know the words of.

TOM HUMPHRIES

If they're going to call you
this superhuman player or
whatever and you believe it,
then you should also believe it
when they call you a tosser.

MARTIN JOHNSON

THERE'S NO 'I' IN 'TEAM'

You have 15 players
in a team. Seven hate
your guts and the
other eight are making
their minds up.

JACK ROWELL

I only get the points because I have teammates who do the work and put me in the position to get them.

JONNY WILKINSON

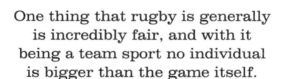

One thing that rugby is generally is incredibly fair, and with it being a team sport no individual is bigger than the game itself.

JEREMY GUSCOTT

Before the game is friendship
– during the game is elegant
violence – after the game
is rugby brotherhood.

ANONYMOUS

———————●●●———————

[Rugby is] a game played by fewer
than 15 a side, at least half of
whom should be totally unfit.

MICHAEL GREEN, *THE ART OF COARSE RUGBY*

Rugby is great. The players don't
wear helmets or padding; they
just beat the living daylights
out of each other and then
go for a beer. I love that.

JOE THEISMANN, AMERICAN FOOTBALLER

• ● •

Remember that rugby is a team
game; all 14 of you make sure
you pass the ball to Jonah.

ANONYMOUS FAX SENT TO THE ALL BLACKS BEFORE THE
1995 WORLD CUP SEMI-FINAL AGAINST ENGLAND

• ● •

Isolate yourself if you
want, but never alone.

CHRISTOPHE PIAZZOLI, FRENCH RUGBY COACH

THE WALLABIES

What's with the Poms
whingeing about the
Wallabies whingeing?
They do more whingeing
about our whingeing than
what we actually whinge.

LETTER TO THE EDITOR OF *THE SYDNEY MORNING HERALD*

Losing to New South Wales is like masturbating, or losing a golf ball. You feel really remorseful afterwards but you know it will happen again if you're not careful.

CHRIS 'BUDDA' HANDY, AUSTRALIAN RUGBY PLAYER

Good on you pasty-faced, transparent-legged geriatric Poms. Your bunch of doddery old geezers showed us how Test matches are won, and we showed you how Test matches are lost.

PATRICK INNES, AUSTRALIAN WRITER

Next weekend is going
to be a tough one,
whatever happened
against New Zealand.
Australia are a different
bag of hammers.

EDDIE O'SULLIVAN

In every facet of the game, we're a bee's dick in front. Why have we Aussies won six of the last eight matches against the All Blacks? Because we're smarter.

UNNAMED WALLABY IN THE *SYDNEY STAR TIMES*

———•◦•———

The impression I get from the guys is that they are happy to tour Europe, but certainly not Afghanistan or Pakistan.

PAT HOWARD, AUSTRALIAN RUGBY PLAYER AND COACH

I once dated a famous Aussie
rugby player who treated me
just like a football: made a pass,
played footsie, then dropped
me as soon as he'd scored.

KATHY LETTE, AUSTRALIAN AUTHOR
AND NEWSPAPER COLUMNIST

UNION V LEAGUE

Look, I'm going
to union and you
can't stop me.

SCOTT QUINNELL, WELSH RUGBY PLAYER

To play rugby league you need three things: a good pass, a good tackle and a good excuse.

ANONYMOUS

———•●•———

League is much, much more physical than union, and that's before anyone starts breaking the rules.

ADRIAN HADLEY, WELSH RUGBY PLAYER

Rugby league is war
without the frills.

ANONYMOUS

———•●•———

It's the first time I've been cold
for seven years. I was never
cold playing rugby league.

JONATHAN DAVIES, ON *A QUESTION OF SPORT*, TALKING
ABOUT RETURNING TO RUGBY UNION IN 1995

I'm 49, I've had a brain
haemorrhage and a triple bypass
and I could still go out and play
a reasonable game of rugby
union. But I wouldn't last 30
seconds in rugby league.

GRAEME LOWE, NEW ZEALAND RUGBY COACH

If loving rugby league's wrong,
I don't want to be right.

JOHN SHARP, MEMBER OF THE UNIVERSITY OF
SHEFFIELD OLD BOYS RUGBY LEAGUE CLUB

Anyone who doesn't watch rugby league is not a real person.

JOHN SINGLETON, AUSTRALIAN ENTREPRENEUR

———•●•———

I like rugby league the most, but I never played it.

STEVE WAUGH, AUSTRALIAN CRICKETER

———•●•———

The sooner that little so-and-so goes to rugby league, the better it will be for us.

DICKIE JEEPS ON GARETH EDWARDS

Rugby league is a simple game played by simple people. Rugby union is a complex game played by wankers.

LAURIE DALEY, AUSTRALIAN RUGBY PLAYER

● ● ●

Anyone who's seen the Wigan [league] players stripped has been faced with the raw truth of the matter... No time for male modelling, and even Princess Di would think twice about getting too close to that lot.

COLIN WELLAND, ENGLISH ACTOR AND SCREENWRITER, *THE OBSERVER*

In south-west Lancashire, babes
don't toddle, they side-step.
Queuing women talk of 'nipping
round the blindside'. Rugby league
provides our cultural adrenalin.
It's a physical manifestation of our
rules of life, comradeship, honest
endeavour, and a staunch, often
ponderous allegiance to fair play.

COLIN WELLAND

The main difference between
playing league and union is
that now I get my hangovers on
Monday instead of Sunday.

TOM DAVID, WELSH RUGBY PLAYER

My Life as a
Hooker

When a Middle-Aged Bloke
Discovered Rugby

'If this is what a midlife crisis does for you, I want one.'
Luke Benedict, rugby writer for the *Daily Mail*

Steven Gauge

MY LIFE AS A HOOKER
When a Middle-Aged Bloke Discovered Rugby

Steven Gauge

£8.99

Paperback

ISBN: 978-1-84953-211-2

'funny yet so true' Rugby World

Steven Gauge's response to an impending midlife crisis didn't involve piercings, tattoos or a red sports car – instead, he decided to take up rugby. What he found on the pitch was a wonderful game, far removed from the professional televised glamour of international rugby, where ordinary blokes with ordinary jobs (and some extraordinary bellies) get together once in a while and have a great time rolling around in the mud.

By the end of his first few seasons, Steven had cracked his nose and various other parts of his anatomy – but he had cracked the game too, and found a place in the club as Captain of the Fourths.

FOOTBALL

Wit

QUIPS AND QUOTES FOR THE FOOTBALL FANATIC

AUBREY MALONE

FOOTBALL WIT
Quips and Quotes for the Football Fanatic

Aubrey Malone

£9.99
Hardback
ISBN: 978-1-84953-459-8

Football is a game with 22 players,
two linesmen and 20,000 referees.
Bob Monkhouse

I used to play football in my youth but then
my eyes went bad so I became a referee.
Eric Morecambe

When you're finished explaining the offside rule, shouting at the ref and perfecting your ball skills, treat yourself to a hearty half-time chuckle with this premiere collection of footy wise-cracks. No matter if your team win, lose or draw, *Football Wit* will keep you smiling through all the own goals and red cards that come your way.

CRICKET

Wit

QUIPS AND QUOTES FOR THE CRICKET-OBSESSED

RICHARD BENSON

CRICKET WIT
Quips and Quotes for the Cricket-Obsessed

Richard Benson

£9.99

Hardback

ISBN: 978-1-84953-462-8

*Cricket is the greatest game that the wit
of man has yet devised.*
Pelham Warner

Cricket is battle and service and sport and art.
Douglas Jardine

Whether or not you can tell your dibbly-dobblies from your nurdles, this marvellous offering is bound to bowl you over. Crammed full of hilarious quotations from cricket capers worldwide, it's the perfect all-rounder for any fan of the gentleman's game.

If you're interested in finding out more about our books, find us on Facebook at **Summersdale Publishers** and follow us on Twitter at **@Summersdale**.

www.summersdale.com